Shopping for Food

Ruth Thomson

Schools Library and Information Services

Note for parents and teachers

The Changing Times series is soundly based on the requirements of the History Curriculum. Using the device of four generations of a real family, the author combines reminiscences of this family with other people's oral evidence. The oral history is matched with photographs and other contemporary sources. Many other lessons are hidden in the text, which practises the skills of chronological sequencing, gives reference to a timeline and introduces the language and vocabulary of the past. Young children will find much useful information here, as well as a new understanding of the recent history of everyday situations and familiar things.

This edition 2004

Franklin Watts
96 Leonard Street
London EC2A 4XD

Franklin Watts Australia
45–51 Huntley Street
Alexandria
NSW 2015

Copyright © 1992 Franklin Watts

Editor: Sarah Ridley
Designer: Michael Leaman
Educational consultant: John West

A CIP catalogue record for this book is available from the British Library.
Dewey Decimal Classification Number: 381
ISBN 0 7496 5252 7

Acknowledgements: The author and publishers would like to thank the following people and organisations for their help with the preparation of this book: Anthea Shovelton; Lisa Chaney, for her invaluable help and advice; Jim Lawson of The North of England Open Air Museum, Beamish.

Printed in Malaysia

Contents

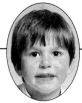
On Saturdays, we go by car
to do our weekly shop
at the superstore.
We buy almost all our food
and household goods there.

Sometimes, Mum goes
to the market to buy fruit
and vegetables.

When we run out of something, in the middle of the week, Mum buys it at the shop round the corner.

Mum buys bread from the local baker.

The milkman delivers our milk every morning.

These are some of the foods we buy.

I asked Mum whether shopping was the same when she was young.

She said,

'My mother walked down to the nearby shops almost every day.'

'She went to the butcher to buy meat.'

'This is the Brand for Quality Lamb'

for roasts, grills & stews
New Zealand Lamb

NEW ZEALAND LAMB
The Best in the World

'She went to the grocer for tea, flour, sugar, cheese and tinned fruit.'

'She bought kippers and other fish at the fishmonger's.'

9

Mum told me that some people delivered food to her house.

'The milk-float delivered milk every day.'

'The grocer delivered big orders of food by van.'

'The baker came twice a week with a big basket on his arm.'

'In summertime, an ice cream van came round, playing a noisy tune.'

Mum now

Mum aged seven in 1964

1975

1950

When Mum was a baby, the first self-service supermarkets opened up.

For the first time, people could help themselves to things, instead of waiting to be served.

Mum said,

'I remember a new supermarket opening near us.'

'Everything we bought was already in a packet.'

I asked my granny to tell me about shopping when she was young.

She said,

'People weren't in a big rush to get their shopping done.

At the grocer's we had to wait our turn to be served.'

'All the food shops had displays in their windows.'

'The shop kept lots of tinned foods
stacked up on the counters.
Sometimes we bought tinned fruit
or a packet of jelly.'

'Many shops
delivered
your order
to the door.'

When my granny was young
there was a war against Germany.
I asked her whether shopping
changed then.

She said,

'When the war started,
some foods became scarce.'

'The government gave everyone
a ration book with coupons inside.
You gave some of the coupons
to the shopkeeper when you paid.'

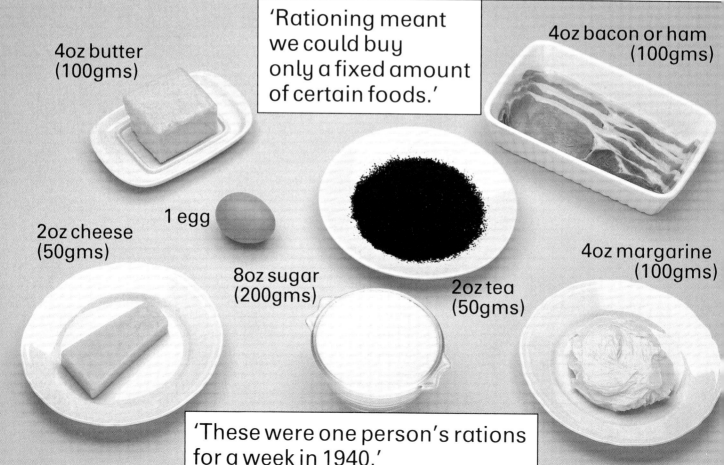

'Rationing meant
we could buy
only a fixed amount
of certain foods.'

4oz butter
(100gms)

4oz bacon or ham
(100gms)

2oz cheese
(50gms)

1 egg

8oz sugar
(200gms)

2oz tea
(50gms)

4oz margarine
(100gms)

'These were one person's rations
for a week in 1940.'

'People stood in long queues
to go shopping.
Even when the war stopped,
there were still queues
and ration books.'

'It was wonderful when
the rationing of sweets
came to an end.'

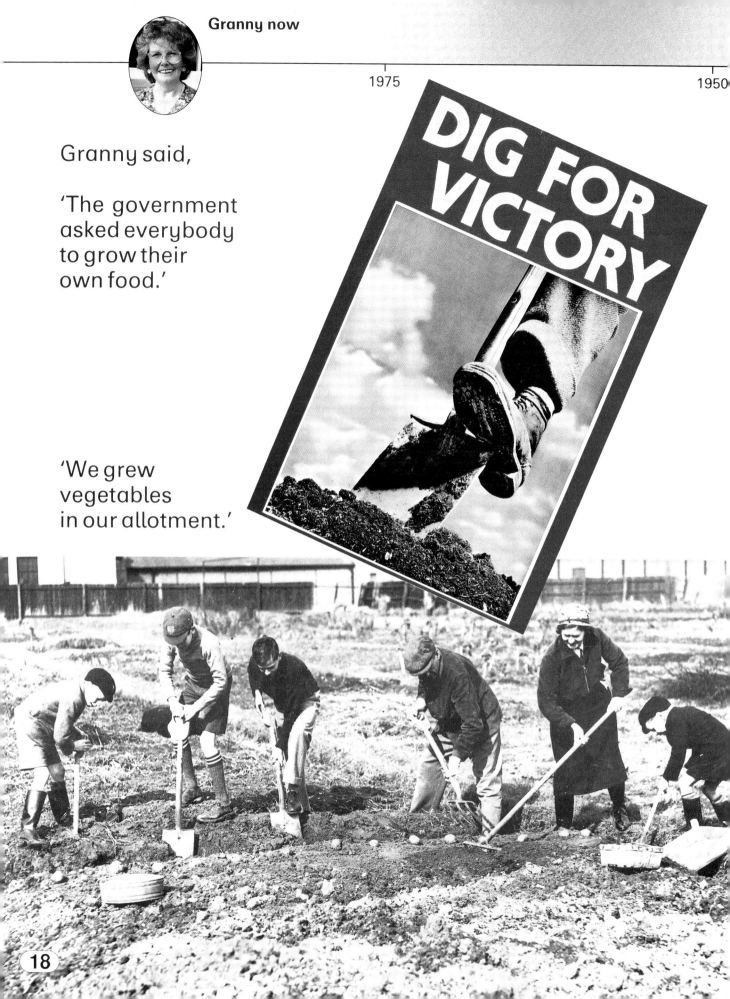

1975   1950

Granny said,

'The government
asked everybody
to grow their
own food.'

'We grew
vegetables
in our allotment.'

DIG FOR VICTORY

'Some families and schools kept chickens, so they could have fresh eggs.'

'Neighbours clubbed together and bought a pig to fatten. They fed it on scraps.'

We want your
KITCHEN WASTE

PIG FOOD

KEEP IT DRY, FREE FROM GLASS, BONES, METAL, PAPER, ETC.
IT ALSO FEEDS POULTRY... YOUR COUNCIL WILL COLLECT

1975   1950

I asked great-granny what sorts of shops
there were when she was young.

She said,

'There were no supermarkets in my day
nor ready-made meals, nor frozen foods.
So everyone went shopping almost every day,
or had food delivered to their house.'

'The milkman came every morning
with a big churn on a cart.
He ladled the milk into jugs
that people brought out to him.'

'The baker's girl came several times a week.
She sold cakes and pies, as well as bread.'

'The grocer came and took a weekly order. An errand boy delivered it on a bicycle with a basket in front.'

Great-granny said,

'We went to lots of different shops to buy our food.'

'We bought fish
at the fishmonger's
and meat at the butcher's.'

'On Saturdays, we sometimes went to the outdoor market.'

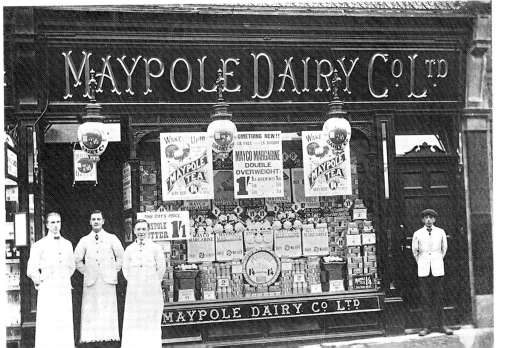

'We bought butter and margarine at the dairy.'

'We went to the grocer's for most other foods.'

Great-granny described
what the grocer's shop was like.
She told me it wasn't full of people
like supermarkets are today.

She said,

'Very few foods were sold in packets,
so you couldn't serve yourself.'

'Shopping took a long time.
You sat down while you waited.'

'A big block of butter was kept
cool on a marble slab.'

'The shopkeeper cut what you wanted,
patted it into shape with wooden pats
and wrapped it in greaseproof paper.'

'Sugar was weighed
on scales
and poured into a bag.'

All the pictures on this page
were taken at a museum.

'The grocer sliced bacon rashers as thick or thin as you wanted.'

'Cheese was cut with a wire from an enormous block.'

'Eggs were laid out on straw in a basket. We bought them in ones or twos.
They were put in a paper bag.'

Things to do

Look at these pictures of shops.
Which ones do you go to?
Which ones do you think your mum,
grandma and great-grandma
went to when they were young?

Look back through the book
to help you.

Make a shopping list of some of the foods
your family buys in a week.
Ask grown-ups to make a shopping list
of foods they ate when they were young.
What is the same? What is different?
Did they buy any of the foods in packets?

Bread

Sugar

Margarine

Flour

Biscuits

Eggs

Cheese

Meat

Sausages

Apples

Potatoes

Carrots

These foods do not grow easily in Britain.
They are brought here fresh, by plane,
and kept cool on their journey.

Ask your parents, grandparents
and other grown-ups whether they remember
any of these foods when they were young.

sweet potato

ginger

mango

avocado pear

aubergine

grapes

red and green peppers

kiwi fruit

Index

Photographs: Beamish title page (t), 15(b), 20, 26(c), 26(b), 27(all); Clarke Foods (UK) Ltd 11(b); Co-operative Society 11(t), 22(b), 28(cl), 28/29; Mary Evans Picture Library 22(t), 28(bl); Chris Fairclough Colour Library 4-5(all), 28(tr); Francis Frith Collection 23(t); Hackney Archives 8(b), 9(b); courtesy of the Trustees of the Imperial War Museum 18(both), 19(both); Peter Millard 6-7, 16(b), 26(tr), 31; National Dairy Council 10; courtesy of New Zealand Meat Producers 8(t); Robert Opie 13(b); Popperfoto 9(t), 17(both); Rank Hovis Ltd 21(t); courtesy of J Sainsbury plc cover(tr) and (bl), endpapers, title page(b), 12, 13(t), 14(both), 21(b), 24-25; Tesco Creative Services 29(b); Topham 16(t); ZEFA cover(br).